ONE

The more the characters depart from what I imagine, the more fun this becomes.

—ONE

Manga creator ONE began *One-Punch Man* as a webcomic, which quickly went viral, garnering over 10 million hits. In addition to *One-Punch Man*, ONE writes and draws the series *Mob Psycho 100* and *Makai no Ossan*.

YUSUKE MURATA

This weekend, I bought baseball gloves for my kids and ended up having more fun than anyone!

—Yusuke Murata

A highly decorated and skilled artist best known for his work on *Eyeshield 21*, Yusuke Murata won the 122nd Hop Step Award (1995) for *Partner* and placed second in the 51st Akatsuka Award (1998) for *Samui Hanashi*.

ONE-PUNCH MAN 13

ONE + YUSUKE MURATA

ONE-PUNCH MAN 13

STORY BY ONE ART BY YUSUKE MURATA

CHARACTERS
BOLTANE
SUIRYU
CHOZE
SOURFACE
ZAKKOS
RING-RING
SAITAMA
STORY
A single man arose to face the evil threatening humankind! His name was Saitama. He became a hero for fun!
With one punch, he has resolved every crisis so far, but no one believes he could be so extraordinarily strong.
Together with his pupil, Genos (Class S), Saitama has been active as a hero and risen from Class C to Class B.
One day, a man named Garo shows up. He admires monsters, so he begins hero hunting and clashes with Metal Bat. Elsewhere, a monster outbreak wreaks havoc, and the heroes struggle to deal with it.
Meanwhile, Saitama has reached the semifinals in a martial arts tournament!

FLASHY FLASH
DEATH GATLING
PEACH TERRY
BONES
RED MUFFLER
SMILEMAN
NARCISSTOIC
TORNADO

MONSTER CELLS

ONE + YUSUKE MURATA

My name is Saitama. I am a hero. My hobby is heroic exploits. I got too strong. And that makes me sad. I can defeat any enemy with one blow. I lost my hair. And I lost all feeling. I want to feel the rush of battle. I would like to meet an incredibly strong enemy. And I would like to defeat it with one blow. That's because I am One-Punch Man.

PUNCH 68: A GREAT FORCE

WHOOOOOM
SMASH BASH
DMMMM
THWAK
WAGH!

WHAM
WHAM
THUD
GLARE
SLITHER
BASH
AGH!
WHOOM

WHSH

KONK

SLITHER
BWAM

YOU ALL RIGHT?
BWOOOM
YEAH, TH-THANKS ...
KRIK
KRAK
Class B, Rank 77
BONES

URGH!
KTOOOM
IT'S WIPING US OUT JUST BY FLOPPING AROUND!
SLITHER

EVEN IF WE MANAGE TO DODGE ...
TNK TNK
TNK TNK
...OUR ATTACKS DON'T WORK!

HUFF
HUFF
...

SLITHER
KRUNK
KRUNK
SPLASH
THAT OCTOPUS IS EATING BUILDINGS AND ELECTRICAL POLES TO GROW LARGER AND TOUGHEN ITS HIDE.

AND THE EYES COVERING ITS BODY CATCH OUR EVERY MOVE.
HAS THERE EVER BEEN A MONSTER THIS STRONG?

NAY!
THIS GIANT OCTOPUS IS HUMANITY'S GREATEST ENEMY EVER!

ALL RIGHT ALREADY! JUST THINK OF A WAY TO BEAT IT!
IT BEAT EVERYONE ELSE, SO WE'RE THE ONLY ONES LEFT!

DO NOT WORRY, RED MUF-FLER.
LEAVE IT TO ME.

HUP
WHAT THE?! BONES!
WHAT CAN YOU DO ALONE ?!

I WILL DEFEAT THAT OCTO-PUS...
...AND EARN A PLACE IN *ETERNAL LEGEND*.
MILK

DON'T WORRY. I CAN WIN.
THIS IS ACTUALLY SORTA LUCKY!

LOOK.
THERE'S AN OVERTURNED MILK TRUCK.
MILK

?
TUMP

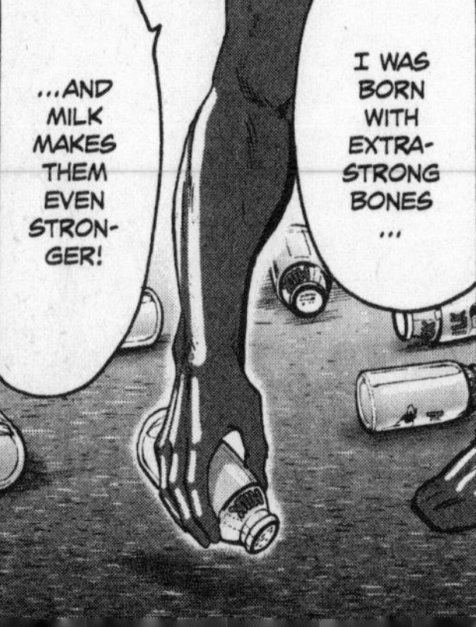
I WAS BORN WITH EXTRA-STRONG BONES...
...AND MILK MAKES THEM EVEN STRON-GER!

GULP
IF I DRINK ALL THIS MILK...
...I WILL BE UNIMAG-INABLY TOUGH!
GULP
GULP
GULP
GULP

THWOK

ACK!

Whole-body fracture

HE WAS TOO HASTY.
!
KTUNK
WHAT'S MOST NECESSARY IN WAR...
...ISN'T STRENGTH OR BONE DENSITY.
IT'S THE ABILITY TO *THINK* AND MAKE *DECISIONS* IN EXTREME CIRCUMSTANCES!

!!!

Class A, Rank 16
BUTTERFLY DX

Class A, Rank 27
SMILEMAN

Class A, Rank 29
NARCISSTOIC

Class A, Rank 30
PEACH TERRY

Class A, Rank 36
CHAIN TOAD

ALL TOGETHER! AIM FOR THE EYES!
IT'S PAYBACK TIME!!
Class A, Rank 8
DEATH GATLING

SIX CLASS-A HEROES?!
THIS JUST MIGHT WORK!

DON'T EVEN BOTHER.

A MEDIOCRE FORCE LIKE THIS...
...WILL JUST UPSET THE OCTOPUS AND CAUSE MORE DAMAGE.
TAK

MEDIOCRE ...?

FLASHY FLASH!
ARE YOU SAYING...

...YOU CAN
FIGHT IT
ALONE?!

SHUT
UP AND
WATCH.

EYES ARE THE WEAK POINT OF ANY LIVING CREATURE.
ANALYSIS ISN'T EVEN NECES-SARY.
!

THEN WE SHOULD COOPER-ATE AND—
FWOOSH
MILK

BOOOSH
MILK

HUH ?!

SPURT

THADOOM

RRM MMMMMM

WHAM

GUSSHH!

WHSH

HE REALLY IS FLASHY!!

THWAM

NO, IT'S...
IT'S THRASHING AROUND!!
THE DAMAGE TO ITS EYES HURT IT!!
GWOARR!!
KWOOM
WHAM
THOOM

UWAAAAAAH!
WHAM
AGH! IT'S NOT STOPPING!

URGH! WE GOTTA RETREAT!!
GNSH
GYAH!

DATATATATA
SK REE!
WHOK
SPAK SPAK SPAK
WHOK
GROOOAR
IT W-WORKED!!
I JUST HIT ITS WOUNDS!

...

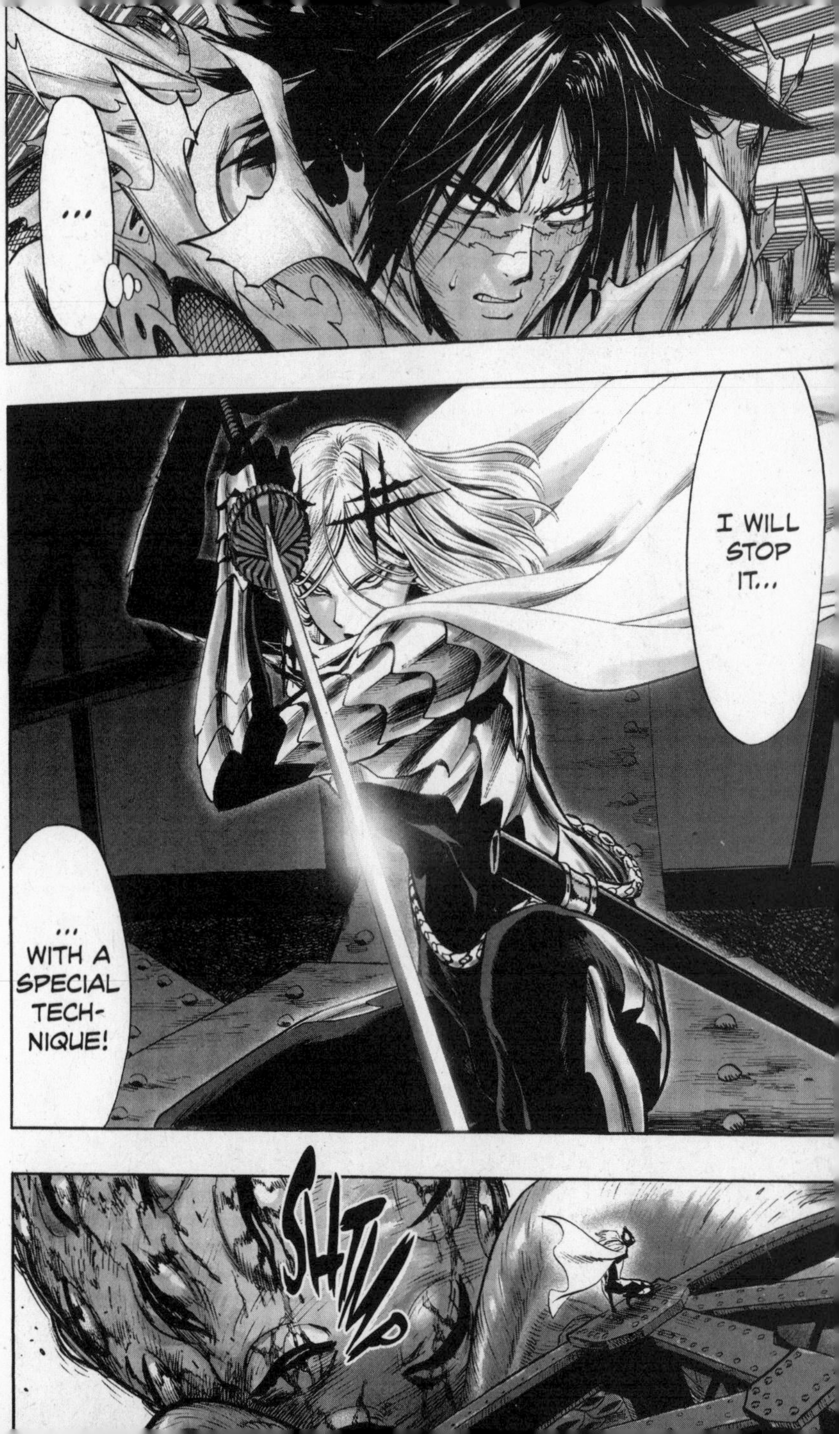

I WILL STOP IT...
... WITH A SPECIAL TECH-NIQUE!

BLOMP

KRRUNKK
GWUP

IT'S THE TERRIBLE...

...TORNADO!

TOMP

GRNCH
KRAK
CRUNCH
SNAP SNAP
SPURRRT
SNAP
KRAK
KRUNNCH

GUSHSHHH
SHHHHH
SHE CRUSHED IT LIKE A TIN CAN!
GWIP
SPLASH
SPLASH

HEY, W-W-WAIT...

SHE'S *DROPPING* IT!
GY-AA-AA-AA-OO-OW!
KABAMMM!!

FSHHHHH...

TH-THAT WAS CLOSE...
WAS SHE *TRYING* TO KILL US?

I HEARD THE RESPONSE WAS SHORT ON HANDS...

...BUT HERE YOU ALL ARE JUST FOOLING AROUND!!

NO, WE WERE FIGHTING THAT–

SHH! DON'T CROSS HER, MAN...

IF YOU'RE CLASS S, THEN ***ACT*** LIKE IT!!!

AND YOU! FLASHY FLASH!!

SILENCE

I WAS KILLING THAT THING UNTIL YOU BUTTED IN!
!

YOU THINK YOU'RE TOUGHER THAN ME?!
YAAAH!! YAAAH !!!
WHAT IF SHE HEARS YOU?!
LEAVE US OUT OF THIS!!

HWSH
WHAT A BUNCH OF USELESS FOOLS!

I HAVE TO ADMIT WE COULDN'T HAVE WON ON OUR OWN.
URGH... CLASS-A HEROES ARE IN A BAD POSITION!

HMM ...
THAT WAS A FAIRLY STRONG MONSTER ...

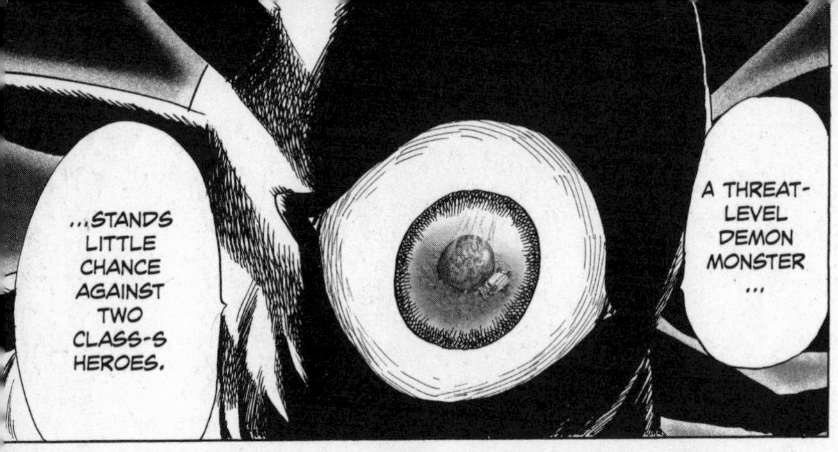
A THREAT-LEVEL DEMON MONSTER...
...STANDS LITTLE CHANCE AGAINST TWO CLASS-S HEROES.

TORNADO IS FORMIDABLE...
YEEN
PERHAPS I SHOULD FACE HER...

DO NOT WORRY.

I CAN MAKE MORE MONSTERS ...

LOOM
SHLING

CANNED PANELS REVEALED!

PUNCH 69: MONSTER CELLS

Deep in the mountains near City G

TODAY'S MEETING IS RUNNING LONG.
MASTER ATOMIC WENT IN THREE HOURS AGO.
Class A, Rank 3
OKAMA ITACHI

THAT'S HOW SERIOUS THIS INCIDENT IS...
EVEN THE *HOLY ORDER OF THE SWORD*...
Class A, Rank 4
BUSHI DRILL

...THE GREATEST WIELDERS OF THE SWORD...
...HAVE DECIDED TO GATHER DURING THIS TIME OF CRISIS.

MASTER SAID HE WILL PRESS FOR THE ORDER TO PARTICIPATE IN DEFEATING THE HERO HUNTER.

IS THE HUNTER REALLY SUCH A THREAT?
Class A, Rank 2
IAIAN

THE HERO HUNTER ...
...IS A BOY NAMED GARO.
HE WAS THE MOST SKILLED OF SILVERFANG'S PUPILS.

THAT'S WHY MASTER ATOMIC IS SO CON-CERNED.
HE VALUES SILVER-FANG'S ABILITY HIGHLY.

THEN, AS MASTER'S FOREMOST PUPIL, *I* SHOULD FACE GARO.

MASTER WOULD BE PLEASED TO SEE I AM STRONGER.

A CONTEST OF SKILL AGAINST AN APOSTATE IS UNNECES-SARY.
BEFORE WE HAVE MORE CASUALTIES, WE MUST FORM A TEAM...
...AND CUT HIM DOWN.

I GUESS SO, BUT...
FWSHH

SPRING MUSTACHIO WAS A GENIUS SWORDSMAN AND PROFESSIONAL HERO FROM ONE OF OUR SCHOOLS...
...BUT THE HERO HUNTER CRUSHED HIM.
剣海山
THUS, THIS IS IMPORTANT TO US.

BUT I CANNOT REACH HIM NOW.

HE EXPELLED HIS LAST STUDENT AND CLOSED HIS DOJO.

HE HAS CUT TIES TO PURSUE THE HERO HUNTER, BUT WHY?

PERHAPS HE IS ASHAMED OF HIS FORMER PUPIL'S ACTIONS.
NICHIRIN

MAYBE HE'S PUTTING HIS AFFAIRS IN ORDER...
...IN PREPA-RATION FOR DYING.
AMAHARE

MAYBE HE FEELS RESPONSIBLE AND IS PREPARING TO SACRIFICE HIMSELF.
ZANBAI

WHATEVER THE REASON, HE TAKES THIS SERI-OUSLY...

...SO THE OPPONENT IS A THREAT.

SILVER-FANG MIGHT LOSE.

...AND SILVER-FANG IS A KIND OLD MAN.
...
HE MAY BE TOO SOFT.

IN DEADLY BATTLE, EVERY MOMENT COUNTS.
WE CANNOT LET THOSE TWO FIGHT.

WE MUST FIND GARO FIRST ...
... AND STRIKE HIM DOWN!

FINDING HIM WILL REQUIRE NUMBERS.
PLEASE, LEND ME YOUR STRENGTH.

VERY WELL.
I WILL MOBILIZE MY PUPILS.

RELYING ON US INSTEAD OF THE HERO AS-SOCIATION IS THE RIGHT MOVE.
IT'S TOO DANGEROUS FOR AMATEURS TO FACE AN EXPERT IN FIST OF FLOWING WATER.

WE ARE WORTH A THOU-SAND MEN.
SO WE NEED NOT WORRY.

THANK YOU. SOMEDAY I WILL REPAY YOUR–

IS THIS BORING CONVERSATION OVER YET?

HARA-GIRI...
...YOU ARE DRUNK.
WERE YOU *BORED*?

DID YOU REALLY CALL ME HERE TO PRATTLE ON...
...ABOUT HELPING SOME OLD ACQUAIN-TANCE?
WA HA HA... HEH HEH HOO...
MAYBE *YOU'RE* THE SOFT ONE!

IF HIS FORMER PUPIL OFFS HIM...
...THEN IT JUST SHOWS HE WAS WEAK.

OR DO I ADDRESS THE SUPERHERO *ATOMIC SAMURAI*?
HEH HEH HEH ...
HARAGIRI

WHAT WE *SHOULD* BE SEEKING IS NOT FRIENDSHIP OR WEALTH...
...BUT ONLY THE PURSUIT OF OUR SKILL.
THE STRENGTH OF THE SWORD HAS CARRIED US FAR.
OUR ORDER EXISTS FOR ENCOURAGING COMPETITION.
BUT NOW WE'RE JUST *BUDDIES*?
THAT IS ENOUGH.
YOU DRINK TOO MUCH.
WELL, SHALL WE ADJOURN?
NOT SO FAST.
I'VE GOT SOMETHING TO TALK ABOUT.
SOMETHING *REAL SPECIAL*!

PULSE
WHAT ARE THOSE?
PULSE

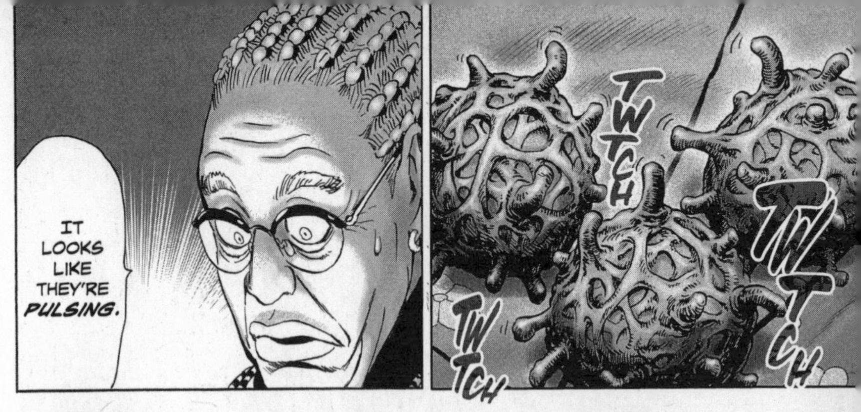

THEY'RE *MONSTER CELLS*.

TAKING ONE WITHIN YOUR BODY...

... RESULTS IN SUPER-HUMAN STRENGTH AND A LONGER LIFE SPAN.

SWIP
IN OTHER WORDS, YOU BECOME A *MONSTER*.

YOU SPEAK APOSTASY.
HE'S POISED TO STRIKE ...
WHERE DID YOU GET THESE?

THERE'S A GROUP CALLED THE *MONSTER ASSOCIATION*, AND IT OPPOSES THE *HERO ASSOCIATION*.
THEY REACHED OUT TO ME THE OTHER DAY.
AND I JOINED THEM, FORFEITING MY HUMANITY IN RETURN FOR GREATER STRENGTH.

OR... YOU ARE JUST DRUNK.
LAY DOWN YOUR BLADE.
THE JOKE ENDS NOW.

BLOG
YOU PUT THIS IN YOUR BODY?

THAT'S RIGHT!

AND UNBELIEV-ABLE POWER FILLED ME!
THE VERY POWER I SOUGHT!
BWORRMPH

I AM NO LONGER HUMAN!
KRRRK
I CAN DECAPITATE ALL FOUR OF YOU RIGHT NOW!
KRAK
SNAP

YES, I HAVE!

AND YOU MUST BECOME MONSTERS TOO!
HUH ?!

WE'LL BE THE DEMONIC ORDER OF THE SWORD ...
...AND ATTAIN NEW HEIGHTS!

IS THAT AN ORDER FROM THE MONSTER ASSOCIA-TION?
YOU HAVE FALLEN LOW, HARA-GIRI.
HEH HEH HEH ...
BE CAREFUL. YOU'RE WITHIN RANGE OF MY SWORD.

KNOW THIS!
I ALWAYS DREW MY BLADE FASTER THAN SOUND ...
... AND NOW I'M EVEN FASTER!

I'LL TAKE ALL YOUR HEADS OFF AT ONCE!
I'M DISAPPOINTED AT HOW EASILY I GOT THE DROP ON YOU.
AND I KILL THOSE WHO REFUSE ME!
THIS IS SAD.
YES, UNFORTUNATELY FOR YOU, ATOMIC SAMURAI...
...I WAS TOLD TO KILL YOU EITHER WAY.

I WILL WAIT ...
... THREE SECONDS!
EAT THE MONSTER CELLS!
THREE ...
... TWO ...
... ONE!
PING
WE ARE NOT AS DUMB AS YOU!

BWASH

SWISH

SPWASHHH

IAIAN... THE HERO HUNTER IS NOT THE ONLY PROBLEM.

WE WILL *ALL* ADDRESS THIS.

AND WE WILL FIRST CRUSH THE *MONSTER ASSOCIATION*!

MONSTER ASSOCIA-TION...

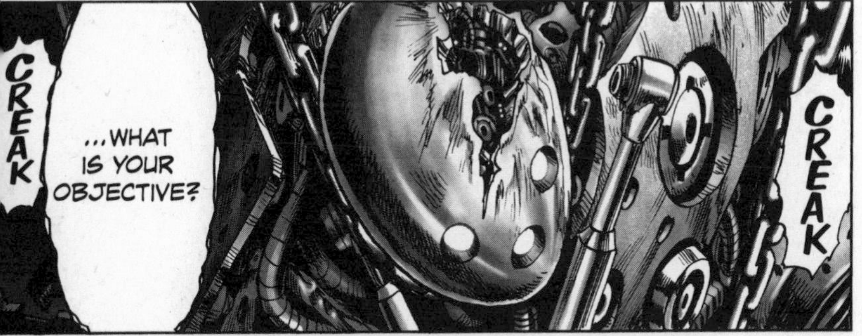
CREAK
...WHAT IS YOUR OBJECTIVE?
CREAK

PURE DESTRUCTION AND CARNAGE?

VIOLENCE IS A FUNDAMENTAL DESIRE OF MONSTERS...

...BUT THAT IS NOT OUR GOAL.

WE ARE TRYING TO ATTAIN A HIGHER STAGE.

IF YOU KEEP WATCHING, YOU WILL WITNESS...

RAAAAAAH

SCRITCH

SCRATCH

TCH... THIS CHEAP WIG IS NO GOOD.

IT'S UNCOMFORTABLE AND MAKES MY HEAD ITCHY.

KACH
AK
HEY! YOU'RE ON!!
FOMF

WHY YA HOLDIN' YOUR HEAD?
YOU NERVOUS?
UH, YEAH.

SUIRYU'S MATCH WAS AMAZING.
BOLTANE'S STRONG, BUT ONE KICK TOOK HIM DOWN.
YOU MIGHT FACE HIM FOR THE CHAMPION-SHIP!

BUT YOUR OPPONENT IN THE SEMIFINALS IS NASTY TOO!
HE MIGHT EVEN WIN THE TOURNAMENT!

BE CAREFUL, CHARANKO!

HE'S BEING SO NICE, BUT I'M NOT CHARANKO...

AND THE SEMIFINALS CONTINUE!

PAY ATTENTION TO THIS MATCH!

RAAAAH

RAAAAAH

CHOZE OF THE CHOSEN-ONE WAY...

...WHO HAS RISEN THROUGH THE PHYSICAL DESTRUCTION OF HIS OPPONENTS!

VERSUS!

CHARANKO OF THE FIST OF WATER POLO, CARBONATION...

...WHO HAS WON ALL HIS MATCHES WITH ONE PUNCH!

BUT DOING THAT'S *EASY*.

I'M ON A WHOLE OTHER LEVEL. I TAKE MY TIME WHEN SERVING AN *EXECUTION*.

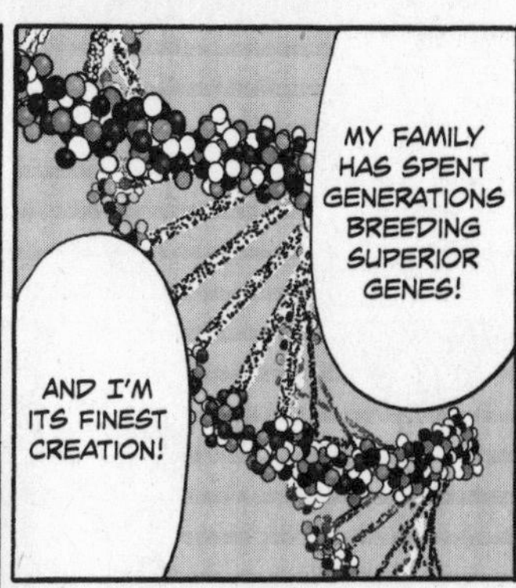

YOU'RE GONNA DIE.
I CAN'T WAIT TO SEE YOU WEEP AND SCREAM.
THE MATCH BEGINS!

KA
YAWN
THOK

YAAAY
...
SUIRYU DEFEATED BOLTANE IN ONLY THREE SECONDS...
...BUT CHARANKO JUST WON IN *TWO* SECONDS!
THE TOURNAMENT'S ALMOST OVER NOW...
WHAT'S GOING ON?
THAT PUNCH ISN'T NORMAL.
WHERE WAS HE BEFORE?
YEAH, IT'S HARD TO BELIEVE ...
HE MIGHT WIN THE WHOLE THING.

THIS IS UNPRECE-DENTED!
NO ONE HAS TOUCHED OUR TWO REMAINING CONTES-TANTS!
RSTL RSTL
AND CHARANKO'S BACKGROUND AND STYLE REMAIN UNREVEALED!

HE'S A TOTAL MYSTERY!

TUMP
WE JUST MIGHT SEE...
...AN UPSET MORE STUNNING THAN BAKUZAN'S DEFEAT!!
AND I CAN TELL THAT'S WHAT THE FANS EXPECT!

BUT THIS MAN STANDS IN HIS WAY!
RAAAH
I CAN'T EVEN *IMAGINE* HIM RUNNING INTO TROUBLE!

IN FACT, IT'S NEVER HAPPENED IN PUBLIC COMPETITION!

KYAAH

KYAAH

SUIRYU!

BEAT 'IM UP!

BUT COULD HIS UNDEFEATED RECORD...

ROOOAR

...FACE ITS FIRST CHAL-LENGE?

IT'S SUIRYU'S DARK CORPOREAL FIST ...
... VERSUS ...
... CHARANKO'S FIST OF WATER POLO!
STARE!!
IT'S THE CHAMPION-SHIP MATCH!
I THINK HE NOTICED MY WIG...

PUNCH 70: STRENGTH IS FUN

RAAH RAAH!
RAAH!
SUIRYU HAS WON EVERY MATCH WITH A SINGLE KICK!
ONE BLOW FROM HIS LONG LEGS IMMEDIATELY RENDERS HIS VICTIMS UNCON-SCIOUS!
SUPER FIGHT 22
RAOOOOAR

RAAH!
RAAH!
RAAH!
MEANWHILE, CHARANKO HAS WON EACH MATCH WITH ONE ROUGH PUNCH!
SUPER FIGHT 22
THEY HAVE DIFFERING STYLES BUT ARE BOTH HEAVY ON OFFENSE!!
ROOOAR

SUIRYU SMILES!
IS HIS WHITE-BELTED OPPONENT WEARING THAT IDIOTIC STARE IN ORDER TO HIDE NERVES?!
DO HIS TECHNIQUE AND EXPERIENCE GIVE HIM AN EDGE?!
THIS IS JUST HOW I LOOK...
READY!
ROOOOAR
CHARAN-KO...

... LET'S HAVE SOME FUN.
GRIN

...
SWEP
FWUF
THAT WAS CLOSE!
WHIP

W-
WHAT'S
THIS?!
SUIRYU
LAUNCHED
THE FIRST
ATTACK...

ROOOOAR
...BUT STOPPED JUST BEFORE CONTACT!
CHARAN-KO IS STUNNED!
THAT KICK WAS SO FAST...
SLO-MO
...WE COULDN'T SEE WHAT HAPPENED !!
ROOOOOOOOAR
TUMP
...
TUMP

BASH

FWUF
!
SWIP

SHOO
IF SUIRYU HAD CONNECTED, THIS MATCH WOULD BE OVER!!

HE STOPPED AGAIN!! HE'S SO FAST I CAN'T SEE HIS MOVES!
OVER-WHELMED, CHARANKO IS BACKING AWAY!
TA
TUMP

SHUP
RAAAH
IS SUIRYU JUST PLAYING AROUND ?!!
I THOUGHT I'D FEEL HIM OUT FIRST...
... BUT THE BREEZE FROM HIS KICKS IS DANGER-OUS!
IS HE AIMING WHERE I THINK HE IS?!
ULP

WHAT'S WRONG?

I'M SURE YOU CAN FOLLOW MY MOVES!

DON'T TELL ME YOU REALLY *ARE* NERVOUS!

BWSH!

BWOOOOSH

THE MATCH HAS BEGUN.

SO STOP FEELING ME OUT ...

...AND FLIP YOUR SWITCH TO ***ON***!

I CAN TELL YOU'RE PRETTY STRONG...

... BECAUSE I AM TOO.

WHY DID YOU JOIN THE SUPERFIGHT?

YOU MUST HAVE A REASON!

I WANT TO HAVE FUN FIGHTING A GOOD OPPONENT.

IT'S NICE TO LIMBER UP SOME-TIMES.

COMPARING MY SKILLS TO SOMEONE STRONG IS FUN!

SKILLED GUYS LIKE YOU ARE HARD TO FIND.

SO THIS IS A FINE DAY.

FUN ...?

YES.

STRENGTH IS *FUN*!

THE STRONGER HUMANS ARE...
...THE FREER THEY BECOME!
THEN YOU CAN LIVE EASY!

BUT SOMETIMES THAT ISN'T ENOUGH...
...SO YOU NEED STIMULATION.

I BET YOU'RE STARVING ...
... FOR A THRILL!
ISN'T THAT WHY YOU CAME HERE?
...
RAAAH

STRENGTH MAKES LIFE EASY, AND FIGHTING STRONG GUYS IS FUN...
STRENGTH IS FUN, HUH?

OH, I GET IT...
HE'S A POSITIVE THINKER!
?

I CAME HERE TO EXPERIENCE MARTIAL ARTS.
I HEARD IT'S TOUGH, SO I WAS INTERESTED.

BUT I ALWAYS WIN IN NO TIME.
WHAT ARE THEY TALKING ABOUT?
I DUNNO. MAYBE ABOUT DA HARD ROAD TA DIS MATCH?
I WAS BEGINNING TO THINK THERE WAS NO POINT IN COMING...

...BUT CONSIDERING THE CROWD'S EXCITEMENT ...

...AND YOUR CONFIDENCE ...

SMIRK

SO HERE'S A SUGGES-TION!

I'LL HELP YOU EXPERIENCE MARTIAL ARTS!

PING

IN RETURN, YOU GOTTA MAKE THIS FUN FOR ME!

GOOD IDEA!

MAYBE I CAN EXPERI-ENCE HOW TOUGH MARTIAL ARTS ARE!

POMF

GREAT!

RAAH

YAAAY

WE HAVE AN AGREE-MENT...

TUMP

HERE I COME!!!

SUIRYU GOT EVEN FASTER!
DID HE FINALLY GET SERIOUS?!
SKRIK
CRUNK

BWSH
WHIP
WHSH
HE DIDN'T STOP THIS TIME! HE CONNECTED!
WITH A *MAS-SIVE* HIGH KICK!!
AND WE COULD HEAR IT ALL THE WAY UP HERE!
BUT CHARANKO IS SUC-CESSFULLY DEFENDING!
HE BLOCKED WITH HIS ARM!! IS IT ALL RIGHT?!
AND NOW FOR SOME *MORE* ...

HYAH!!
HE KICKED HIM INTO THE AIR!

HM?

WHOK
WHOOSH
CHARANKO!!

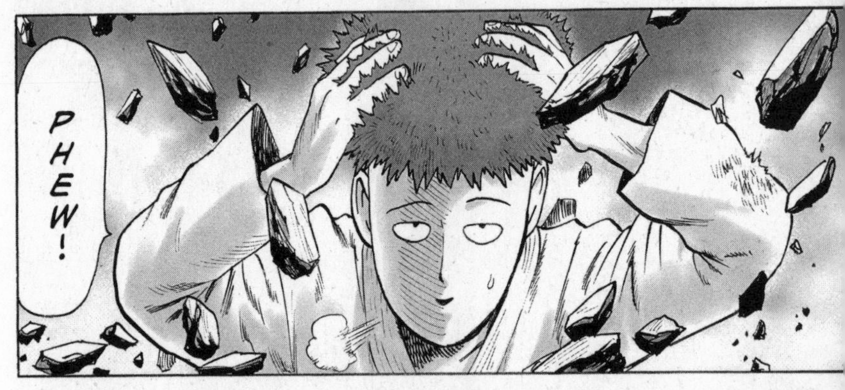

CLUNK
CLUNK
...
UH-OH!!
SWIP

I BET HE CAVED IN CHARANKO'S FACE!

IS CHARANKO ALL RIGHT?!

THE REF SHOULD STOP THE MATCH! IT'S NOT FAIR!!

SWOOSH

CAN HE GET BACK UP?!

TOMP
IS THIS OVER?
YOU WANTED TO EXPERIENCE MARTIAL ARTS, SO I'M NOT HOLDING BACK.
FSHHHH...
YEAH, THAT SCARED ME...
KRNK
MY WIG ALMOST FLEW OFF!

GOOD ...
THAT MAKES THIS MORE FUN!

BA BA BA
BA BA BA
BA BA BA
VWSH

S- SUIRYU ALWAYS WINS HIS MATCHES WITH ONE BLOW...
BABABAM
...BUT CHARANKO'S HANGIN' IN THERE!
MAYBE CHARANKO CAN WIN THIS!
WHAK
NO...
...WATCH SUIRYU CLOSELY.
?!

HE'S ONLY USING LEG MOVES.
I DON'T KNOW WHY...
...BUT HE WANTS TO WIN WITH ONLY KICKS.
HE'S STILL JUST FOOLING AROUND...
THAT COCKY *PUNK*!

WHICH MEANS ...
HE'S HIDING HIS TRUE ABILITY.

BUT HIS OPPO-NENT...

I FEEL LIKE I KNOW HIM...
OR IS IT MY IMAGINA-TION?

YOU USE STRONG PUNCHES, RIGHT?

WHSH

BA BAM

BA BAM

YOU BEAT EVERYONE WITH ONE PUNCH!

ACTUALLY, YOU *SLAPPED* ZAKKOS...

SO COME ON...
...HIT ME WITH A PUNCH!
MAKE THIS FUN!
JOLT

UH-OH!!
VAWOOSH
CHARAN-KO BACKED OFF AGAIN!!
SKRID
SMIRK

HE CAN'T EVEN FIGHT BACK!!

DRIP

BABMP
BABMP
...
BABMP
THAT WAS CLOSE!

DID HE NOTICE I WAS READY TO COUNTER WITH A KICK?
HMM... HE'S GOOD!

...IF YOU DON'T FIGHT BACK, YOU CAN'T WIN!

BABABAM

BUT ...

GA

VWSH

WHOA! ANOTHER CLOSE CALL!!

HE'S SMART. HE ALWAYS GUARDS HIS HEAD...

TATUMP

HOW DO YOU USUALLY SPEND YOUR TIME?
WELL, UM...
...I TAKE WALKS AND FIGHT MONSTERS.

BUT IT'S A WORTHLESS PROFESSION.

I FOUGHT CLASS-A HEROES HERE...
RAAAU
...AND THEY WERE WEAKLINGS.

"HERO" IS JUST A WORD.
BUT HEROES DON'T REALLY EXIST.

YAA AH

GYAAH—
WAAH—
HERO ASSOCIATION HOSPITAL

THOK
SMUSH

UNGH...
TRMBL
TRMBL
GYAAH
WHAM
WAAH—
GYO FOO FOO!

GOOD THING THE HERO HUNTER DIDN'T KILL YOU!
GRIN
NOW I GET THE CRED FOR OFFING A WOUNDED HERO!
Monster
GYOFFERY

INTENSIVE CARE UNIT

THE ICU STILL HAS PATIENTS...

BANG

WHAM

...WHO CAN'T EVACUATE!

I MUST STAND MY GROUND!!!

GYO FOO FOO! OH...

THANKS FOR NOT RUNNIN'!

YOU'RE A BIG CATCH!

GRIP

GYO?

NOW!

GAGH!

STMP

WHAM
TANK-TOP TACKLE!

GYOFOOO!
BKOOM

WOW ...
THAT'S A SERIOUS TACKLE, TANK-TOP MASTER ...
HWOOOOOO

YOU'RE IN BAD SHAPE.
WITHOUT A TANK TOP, YOU SHOULD BE CARE-FUL.
CAN YOU STAND, MUMEN RIDER?

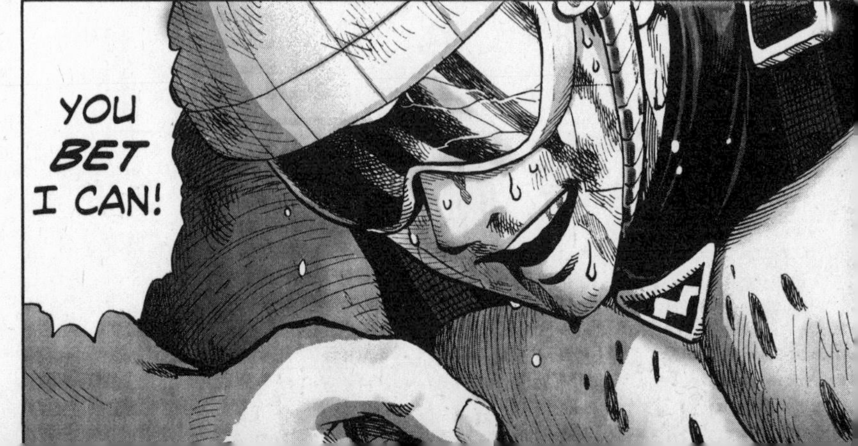
YOU BET I CAN!

IT'S THEIR JOB, BUT HEROES BOAST ABOUT GOOD DEEDS AND JUSTICE!
RAAAH
PEOPLE LIKE THAT WILL NEVER SAVE THE WORLD.

RELYING ON THEM IS POINTLESS.

NOBLE ASPIRA-TIONS...
FINE THOUGHTS ...
LOFTY ETHICS ...
HEROIC JUSTICE ...
ROOOOAAAAAAAR

THOSE AREN'T NECESSARY FOR A FUN LIFE.
OOOOO
THEY'RE JUST BORING CONTAM-INANTS.

YOU'RE STRONG, SO YOU SHOULDN'T DO SOME-THING SO BORING.
RAAAAAAH
CHOOSE A MORE FUN PATH...
...AND RAKE IN THE OCCASIONAL TOURNAMENT WINNINGS!
UH-OH... DID I BUM YOU OUT?

WHOK

THAT WAS A CLEAN HIT!

BUT... WHAT ?!!

YOU'RE NOT THE ONLY ONE DOING WHAT YOU WANT.
NOW I HAVE SOME ADVICE FOR YOU.
FSHHH
IF YOU WANNA HAVE FUN...

...YOU SHOULD AVOID GETTING ANY STRONGER.

WHOOPS... I ALMOST DID IT AGAIN.
THAT WAS CLOSE!

THE MATCH WAS ALMOST OVER TOO SOON!
PHEW

Extra reck-less!
TANK-TOP MUMEN RIDER

PUNCH 71: MARTIAL ARTS IS...!

THIS TIME, *CHARANKO* STOPPED HIS PUNCH JUST SHORT!!!

WHOA A A

DID YOU SEE THAT?!!

WOW! I'VE NEVER SEEN ANYTHING LIKE IT!!

RAAAAH
WHEN SUIRYU'S MUSCLES BULGED, HIS CLOTHES FLEW OFF!!!
HAS HE FINALLY GOTTEN SERIOUS?!!
RAAH

SUIRYU'S UNIFORM BLEW TO SHREDS...
...REVEALING A WELL-HONED BODY OF STEEL!
RAAAH
WILL CHARANKO'S COCKY COPYCAT PROVOCATION...
...FINALLY BREAK SUIRYU'S COOL DEMEANOR?!

AND WE'VE LEARNED A SHOCKING TRUTH ABOUT CHARANKO!
CHTTR
CHTTR
HE WAS WEARING A WIG!!
YAAY
HUBBUB

THE REFS ARE GATHERING...

WHAT DOES THIS MEAN?!
FWUP

THE TOURNAMENT RULES HAVE CHANGED...

...SINCE THE WOLFMAN INCIDENT LAST TIME!

CONTESTANTS MUST FIGHT UNDER THEIR OWN NAMES AND MAY NOT WEAR MASKS OR HEADGEAR!

AN UNDECLARED WIG CONSTITUTES HEADGEAR!

LATER, WE WILL PERFORM AN INVESTI-GATION TO ASCERTAIN...
...WHETHER THIS MAN REALLY IS CHARANKO!
I GOTTA GET OUTTA HERE...

HM? MAYBE IT *IS* WHO I THOUGHT IT WAS!
DO YOU KNOW HIM?

CHARAN-KO WAS WORRIED ABOUT GOIN' BALD?
NO, THAT'S AN IMPER-SONATOR.

HOLY COW!
WHAT A LET-DOWN!
THE MATCH IS OVER !!!

WAA
AND THE VICTOR IS...
...SUIRYU!!!
AAH
HUH?! SERIOUSLY?!
BOOO!
I WANTED TO SEE MORE!
WAAAH!
BOO!
Suiryu was just getting serious!
WAAH
THE ORGANIZERS NEED TO GET A CLUE!
BOO
CONTINUE THE FIGHT!!

IT'S OVER.
ASSEMBLE THE ATHLETES FOR THE AWARD CEREMONY.
ALL RIGHT, I'LL AN-NOUNCE IT RIGHT NOW.
ALSO, THERE'S A MON-STER ALERT ...
...SO TELL EVERYONE TO STAY IN THE VENUE.
YES, OF COURSE.
OH...
SIGHH
...THE FIGHT'S OVER?
PLAY-TIME'S OVER ...
...SO NOW LET'S GET REAL!
RRIP RRIP

HUH?

BASH
URGRAH!
I DON'T CARE *WHO* YOU ARE!
I STILL HAVEN'T SHOWN YOU MY FULL STRENGTH!

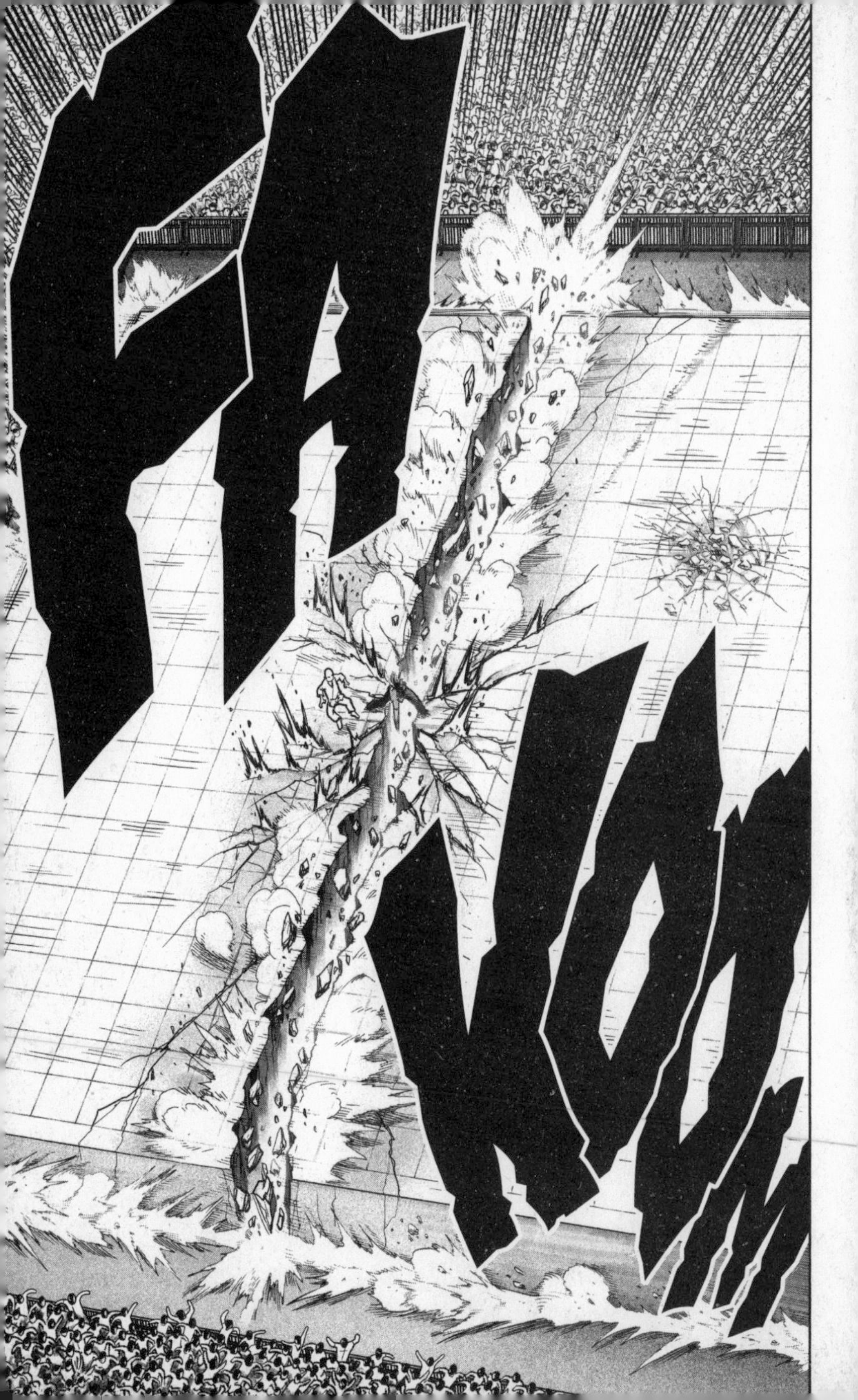

TH...
THE FIGHT PLATFORM SPLIT!!!
YOU'RE NOT GETTING AWAY!

JAKWUNK
HWUP

GR-RA-AA-AA-AH!!!
W-WHAT?! THEY'RE STILL FIGHTING!
THEY'RE GONNA KEEP GOING!

STOMPSTOMPSTOMP
STOMPSTOMP
KTHOOM
...
THWAP
DON'T YOU WANNA HAVE *FUN*?
!

SORRY, BUT I WOULD FEEL LIKE I'D LOST...
SHH
... AND THAT WOULDN'T BE FUN!
STOP! THE FIGHT IS OVER!!
STAFF! SECURITY!! STOP THEM!
S-STOP? THEM ?!
JUST DO IT!
AWE-SOME!! FIGHT!
RAH
FINISH THE FIGHT!
RAH
RAH
SUI-RYU'S SO COOL!
DON'T INTER-FERE, REF!

G R A A A H
THE STAFF'S COMING.
THEN I'LL WIN BEFORE THEY GET HERE!
THIS IS PANDE-MONIUM!
THIS IS KUHHH-RAZY !!!
HEY! DON'T MAKE IT ANY MORE KUHHH-RAZIER ...
SUIRYU IS OVERCOME WITH PASSION!!!
I'VE NEVER SEEN HIM LIKE THIS!!!!
PAY ATTEN-TION WHILE I DEMON-STRATE ...
...TRUE MARTIAL ARTS!
THBABARAM
BABADARAM

DARK BODY FLYING DRAGON FIST!

SUIRYU ATTACKS FROM ABOVE!!
AGAIN!
AND AGAIN !!
BAM BAM BAM
W- WHAT'S GOING ON?!
HE ISN'T ...
BAM
HE ISN'T STOPPING !!
HE'S STILL STRIKING !!!
BAM

GWRRRR

WHAT KIND OF ATTACK IS THAT ?!!!

THAT FACE ...
AM I NOT HAVING ANY EFFECT ?!
IN THAT CASE ...
HUP
... I'LL TRY THIS !!
STOMP

KAK
CREK
CRAK
KA
DARK BODY QUAKE TIGER FIST!
THE PLATFORM ...
...IS FALLING APART!!
TAFF
STA

STOMP
STOMP
STOMP
THAT'S SOME WEIRD FOOT-WORK ...
...FOR STOMPING !!!
FIRM FOOTING CAN INCREASE POWER...
...BUT I'VE NEVER SEEN ANYONE DO *THAT*!
HE'S GETTING VICIOUS!

TRMBL
TRMBL
CCRIK

FWSH

FWMP

STILL NO REACTION?
BUT I COULD SMASH A SEMI WITH THAT!

OKAY, I GET IT.

AHA!

YOU'VE FINALLY REALIZED WHAT MARTIAL ARTS IS?!

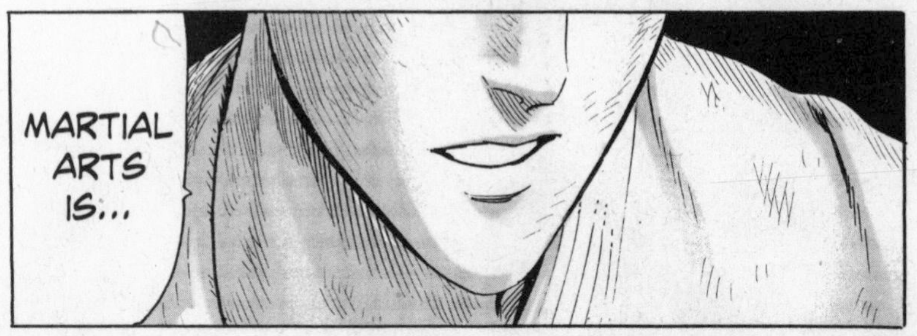

...A WAY TO MOVE ALL COOL-LIKE?

TAKE THIS *SERI-OUSLY!*

WHSH

HM?

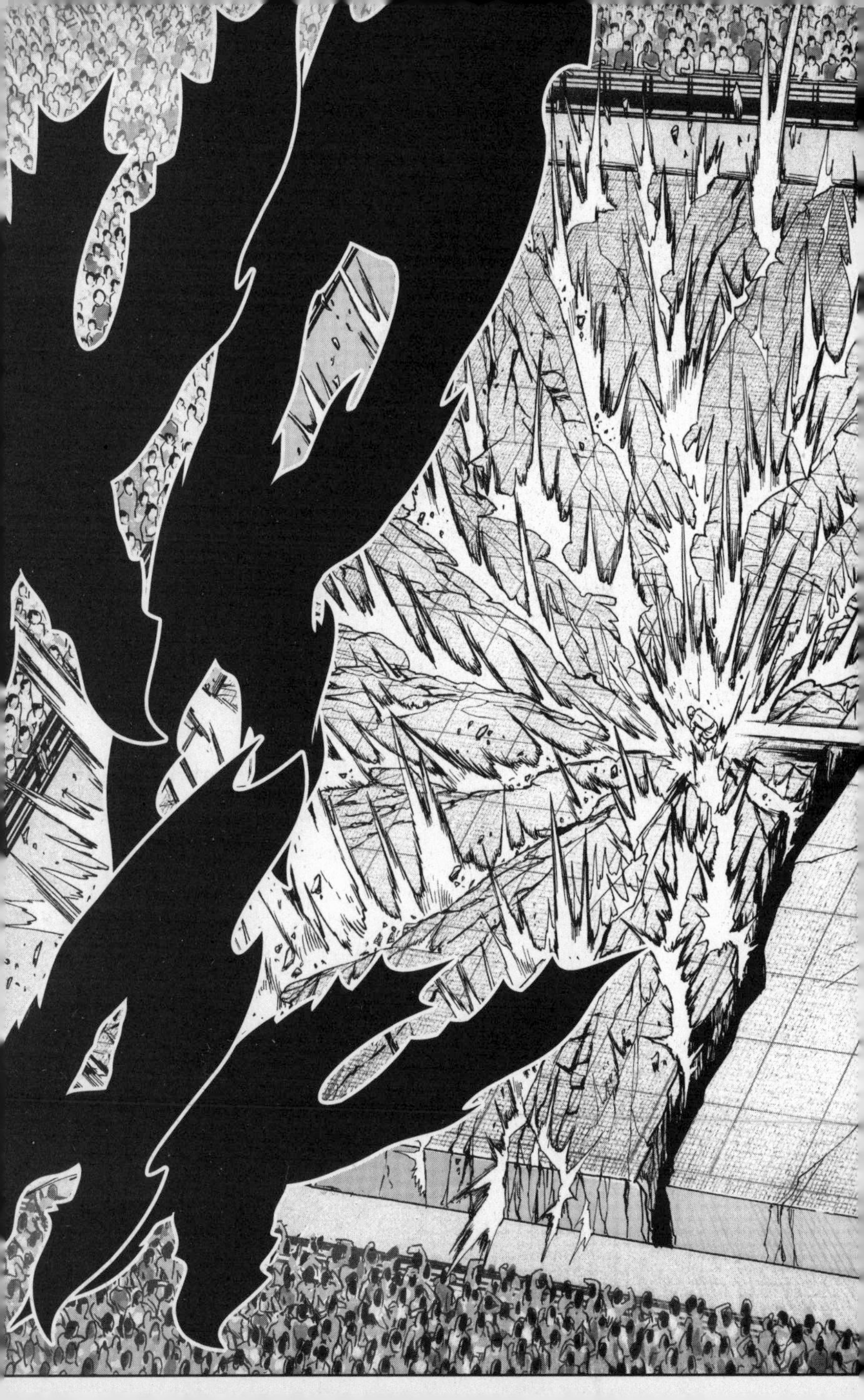

BASH
HE LANDS A BLOW WITH A HIP ATTACK!!
SUIRYU WENT FLYING OUT WITH THE FORCE OF HIS OWN ATTACK!
BUT CHARANKO(?) IS DISQUALIFIED, SO IT DOESN'T COUNT!
KRMBL
KRMBL
OOPS ...
HE TOOK MY BELT...
SLIP

KYAH EEEK
CHARANKO! COVER THAT UP!!
WHY IS SAITAMA HERE?
HUH?

BOO BOO BOO BOO
AW, MAN... HOW UNCOOL ...

AGH! HE RAN AWAY!
STOP RIGHT THERE!!
HE RAN TOWARD THE LOCKER ROOMS! GET HIM!

NOW THAT SUIRYU'S NOT MOVING, THIS IS OUR CHANCE!
SEIZE THAT MAN!
WE'VE GOT TO STOP THEM!
UH-OH ...

...

I JUST LOST...

...FOR THE FIRST TIME.

RAH

RAH

AND NOW FOR THE AWARDS CEREMONY!

ALL ATHLETES WHO ARE STILL MOBILE SHOULD GATHER ON THE PLAT-FORM!

RAH

HURRAY

CONGRATULATIONS ON YOUR WIN, SUIRYU!

THE END WAS A BIT WILD, BUT...

...AS USUAL, YOU REMAINED UNHARMED!!

IF HE HADN'T STOPPED THAT PUNCH...

...WHAT WOULD HAVE HAPPENED TO ME?

HA HA! I KNOW WHAT YOU MEAN!
SUIRYU WILL SAVE US!
I WONDER IF HE'LL SHAKE MY HAND!

I SHOULDN'T WORRY ABOUT IT.
I'LL NEVER SEE THAT GUY AGAIN.
A WIN IS A WIN...
...SO I SHOULD CHILL OUT.
HEY, YOU'RE CUTE.
GOT A BOY-FRIEND?

UH-OH!!!
?
STAFF MEM-BERS HAVE COL-LAPSED!

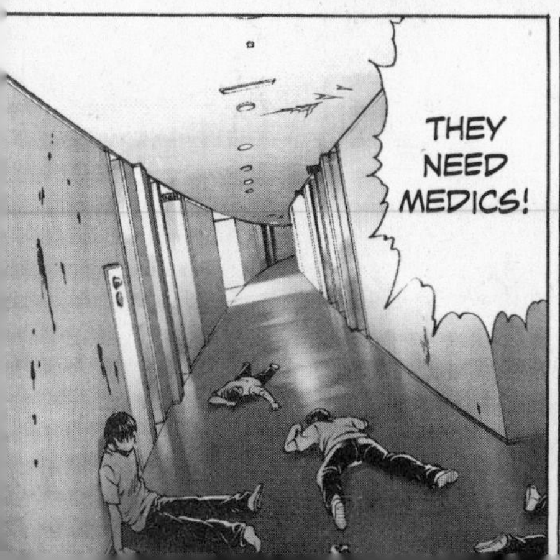
THEY NEED MEDICS!

SOMEONE ATTACKED THEM!

AND SECURITY GUARDS AT THE ENTRANCES TOO!

WHAT ...?

SURELY SAITAMA DIDN'T...

THIS IS NO TIME FOR A CLOSING CEREMONY!!!

KYAAAAH!

LOOK UP THERE!

WAAAAH!

IN THE SKY!!

FWAP

THOMP

RMM MM MMMM MM

M-MONSTERS?!!

DID YOU DO THIS?!!

Threat Level: Demon

THE THREE CROWS

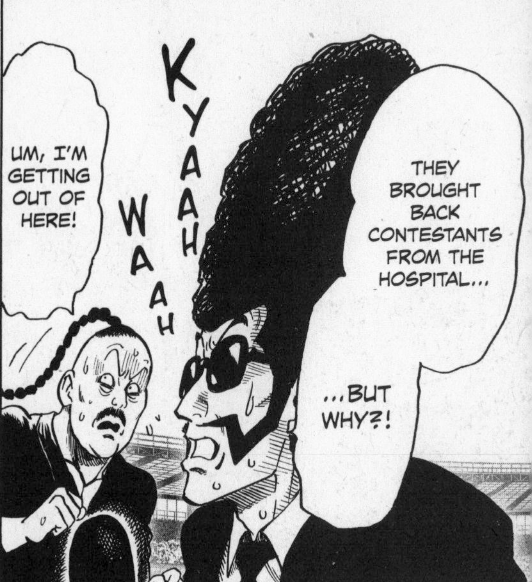
THEY BROUGHT BACK CONTESTANTS FROM THE HOSPITAL...
...BUT WHY?!
KYAAAH
WAAAH
UM, I'M GETTING OUT OF HERE!

I LEAVE THE MON-STERS TO YOU! BYE!
ZOOM
AGH?! HEY!

THAT GUY BENPATS IS RUNNIN' AWAY!

GOOD.

CIVILIANS SHOULD STAY BACK.
SWIP
!
WE PRO HEROES WILL HANDLE THIS!

THOOOM
AGYACK!!!
?!!

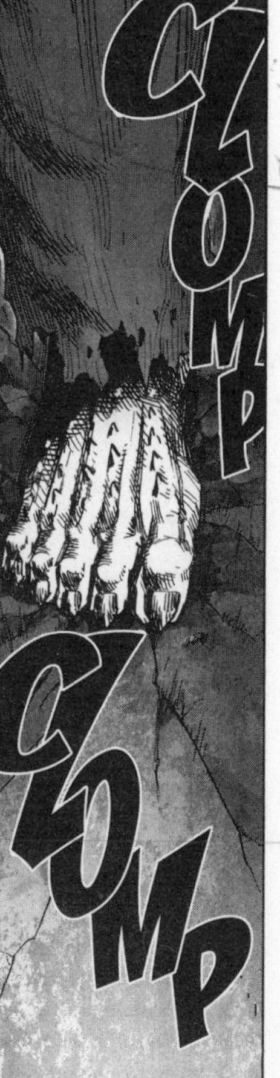

LOOOOOM

KYAAAH
CLOMP
UWAAAH
ARE ALL THE CONTESTANTS HERE?

GOOD. YOU'RE ALL GONNA BE MON-STERS!
Threat Level: Dragon
GOKETSU

CANNED PANELS REVEALED!

TODAY IS THE FINAL DAY OF MY TOUR PROMOTING MY NEW ALBUM.

THANKS TO METICULOUS REHEARSALS, THE STAGE HAS COME ALIVE!

BONUS MANGA: STAR

AND A STELLAR CREW!

BECAUSE OF THEM, I SHINE BRIGHTER THAN ANYONE!

AND AS THE FINALE APPROACHES, I EXPERIENCE AN UNCHARAC-TERISTIC HIGH!

MY BELOVED FANS... WHEN OUR EYES MEET...

...I WISH I COULD EMBRACE YOU ALL, BUT I AM ONLY ONE MAN.

ALL I CAN DO IS SING ABOUT PEACE AND LOVE.

I SWELL WITH THANKFULNESS...

...AND GOODWILL TOWARD ALL LIVING THINGS!

KABOOOOM
?!

KYAAH! DID SOMETHING JUST BREAK IN?!
IS THIS PART OF THE SHOW ?!
Amai Mask

ARE THOSE MONSTERS ?!
THERE ARE PEOPLE ON THE GROUND!

SECURITY GUARDS ...
...AND HEROES!

A MONSTER?! AND IT'S ATTACKING AMAI MASK'S CONCERT ?!
HE STOPPED SINGING, SO IT MUST BE TRUE!
NO WAY!
THIS IS AWFUL!

IS THAT AMAI MASK, A.K.A. HANDSOME KAMEN?

HE'S NUTHIN' BUT GOOD LOOKS.

AND HE'S ONE OF OUR TOP TARGETS.

AS THE FACE OF THE HERO ASSOCIATION, HE'S GOT INFLUENCE.

KYAAAH! AMAI MASK!
THEY CAME FOR YOU!

AMAI!
THEY'RE GONNA ATTACK!

RUUUN!

?!

SWIP

CHATTER CHATTER
HE STARTED SINGING AGAIN...
...BUT WITHOUT THE BAND!
YEAH... IS THIS HIS NEW SONG?
AMAI

IS HE JOKING?!
WHAT SHOULD WE DO, BOSS?
NO, HE'S SERIOUS.
LOOK AT HIS EYES!

HE'S SINGING WHILE LOOKING RIGHT AT THE MONSTERS!

HE WANTS EVEN THEM...
...TO APPRECIATE HIS PERFORMANCE!

HE WANTS TO WIN THIS FIGHT THROUGH *SINGING*!
EH?

HE BELIEVES HE CAN CONVEY A MESSAGE THROUGH HIS SONG...
...AND ESTABLISH A CONNECTION WITH THEM!

...
INCREDIBLE...
HE'S A BONA FIDE SUPER-IDOL!

START PLAYIN', GUYS!
WE BELIEVE IN THE POWER OF MUSIC TOO!

TADAAAAH

NOW HE'S DANCING!
IT EVEN LOOKS CHOREOGRAPHED!
MAYBE THOSE ARE HIS DANCERS IN COSTUME?

GRAB
LET ME HEAR YOU SING IT! ♪
WHAT A GRIP! I CAN'T BREAK FREE!
HE'S STRONG.
I THOUGHT HE WAS JUST A PRETTY FACE.

NOW SHOW ME YOUR MOVES! ♬

FWIP FWIP FWIP

UGH!

HE'S SHOWIN' OFF!

I'M GONNA WIPE THAT SMILE RIGHT OFF HIS FACE!

IF WE KILL YOU, WE'LL BE BIG SHOTS IN THE MONSTER ASSOCIATION!

YOU CAN RESUME SINGING *IN THE AFTERLIFE!*

CAREFUL.

DAMAGING MY FACE WOULD UPSET MY FANS.

FIGHTING IS POINTLESS...

BUT YOU INTER-RUPTED MY CONCERT ...
...SO NOW YOU MUST DIE.

AMAI MASK

AMAI MAA-ASK!
YOU'RE SO COOL! SO PER-FECT! ♡
AND DREAMY TOO!

LOOK AT THAT SMILE!
PHEW... I GUESS IT ***WAS*** ALL JUST FOR SHOW!

THOSE MONSTERS WERE A SURPRISE ...
...BUT THE TOUR WAS STILL A SUCCESS.
IS AMAI ALL RIGHT? HE HASN'T LEFT HIS DRESSING ROOM.
MAYBE THE MONSTERS UNSETTLED HIM?

IT'S NO USE GUESSING. WE CAN'T UNDERSTAND HIM.
WE ONLY KNOW AMAI MASK THE IDOL.

AS A HERO, HE'S BEYOND OUR GRASP.

AMAI MASK

HMM... THE MONSTER ASSOCIATION?

SOUNDS LIKE IT'S TIME FOR ME TO TAKE THE STAGE!

13 Monster Cells (End)

END NOTES

PAGE 58, PANEL 3:

The text on the bottle reads "Sword Sea Mountain," which is a play on the name of a famous brand of sake.

ONE-PUNCH MAN

VOLUME 13

SHONEN JUMP MANGA EDITION

STORY BY | ONE
ART BY | YUSUKE MURATA

TRANSLATION | JOHN WERRY
TOUCH-UP ART AND LETTERING | JAMES GAUBATZ
DESIGN | SHAWN CARRICO
SHONEN JUMP SERIES EDITOR | JOHN BAE
GRAPHIC NOVEL EDITOR | JENNIFER LEBLANC

First published in Japan in 2012 by SHUEISHA Inc., Tokyo.
English translation rights arranged by SHUEISHA Inc.

Printed in the U.S.A.

Published by VIZ Media, LLC
P.O. Box 77010
San Francisco, CA 94107

10 9 8 7 6 5 4 3 2 1
First printing, March 2018

www.viz.com

SHONEN JUMP

www.shonenjump.com

PARENTAL ADVISORY
ONE-PUNCH MAN is rated T for Teen and is recommended for ages 13 and up. This volume contains realistic and fantasy violence.

ratings.viz.com

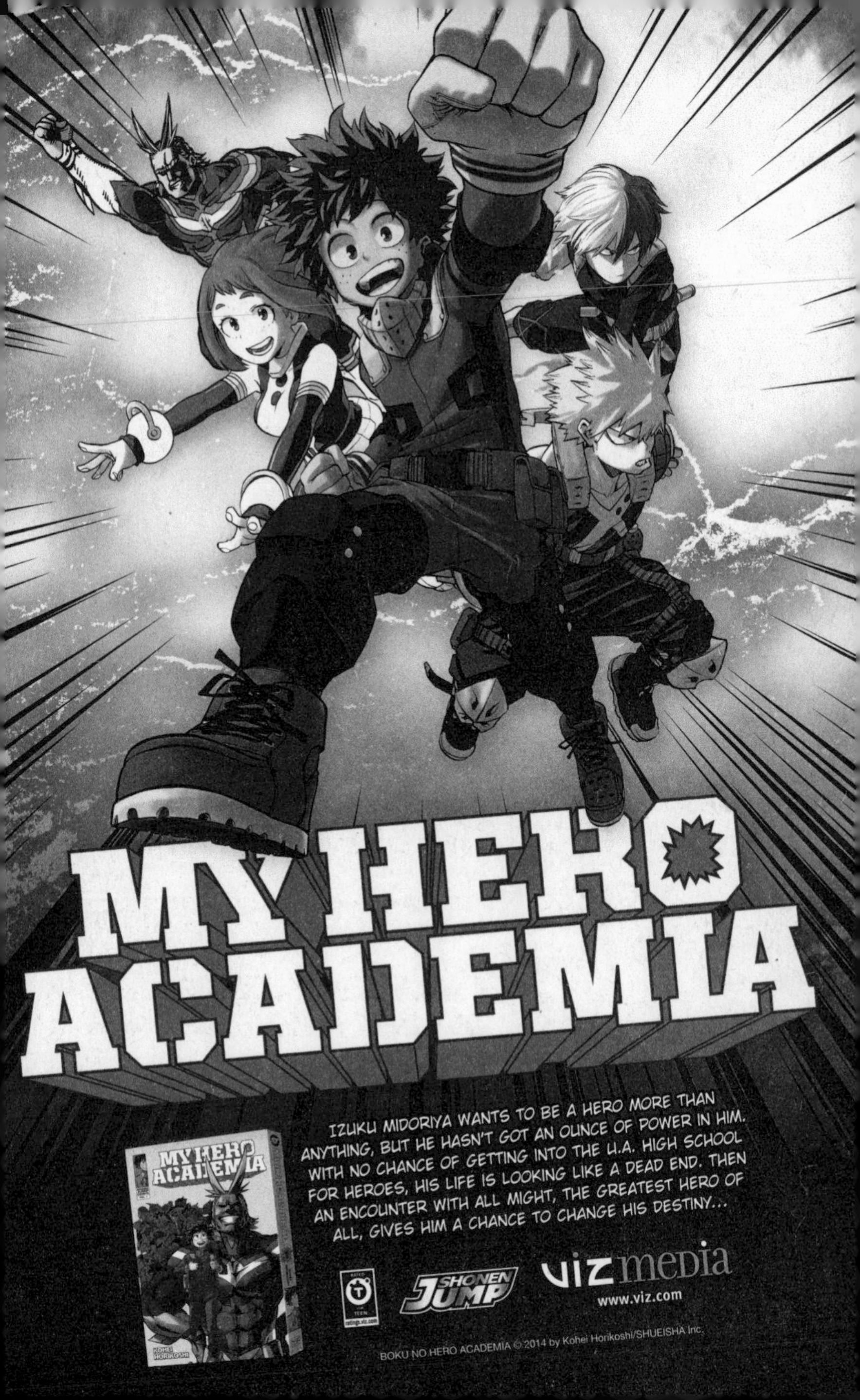

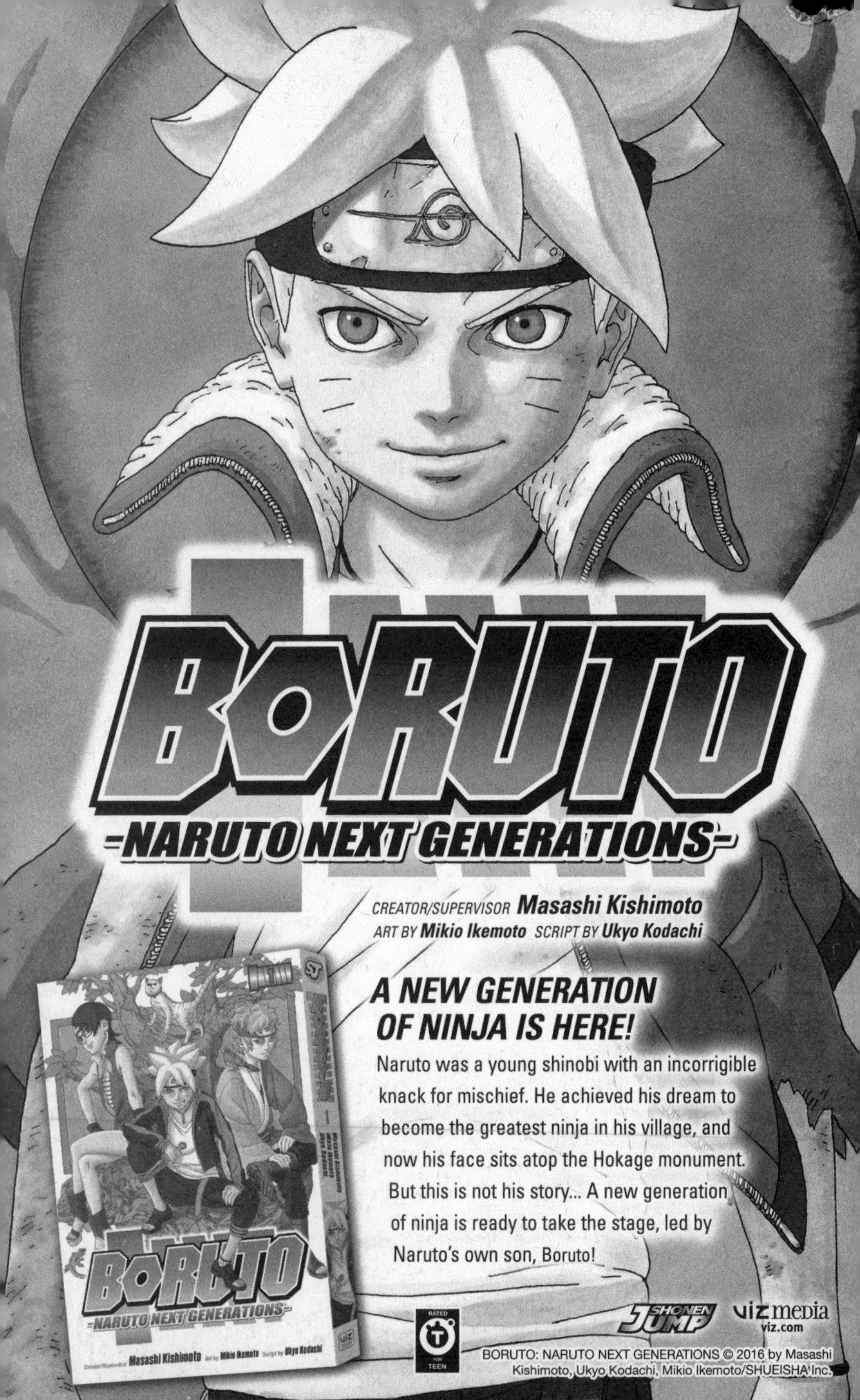
BORUTO
-NARUTO NEXT GENERATIONS-
CREATOR/SUPERVISOR Masashi Kishimoto
ART BY Mikio Ikemoto SCRIPT BY Ukyo Kodachi
A NEW GENERATION OF NINJA IS HERE!
Naruto was a young shinobi with an incorrigible knack for mischief. He achieved his dream to become the greatest ninja in his village, and now his face sits atop the Hokage monument. But this is not his story... A new generation of ninja is ready to take the stage, led by Naruto's own son, Boruto!
BORUTO
-NARUTO NEXT GENERATIONS-
Masashi Kishimoto Mikio Ikemoto Ukyo Kodachi
RATED T FOR TEEN
SHONEN JUMP
viz media
viz.com
BORUTO: NARUTO NEXT GENERATIONS © 2016 by Masashi Kishimoto, Ukyo Kodachi, Mikio Ikemoto/SHUEISHA Inc.

DRAGON BALL SUPER
STORY BY Akira Toriyama ART BY Toyotarou
Goku's adventure from the best-selling classic manga *Dragon Ball* continues in this new series written by Akira Toriyama himself!
Ever since Goku became Earth's greatest hero and gathered the seven Dragon Balls to defeat the evil Boo, his life on Earth has grown a little dull. But new threats loom overhead, and Goku and his friends will have to defend the planet once again!
RATED T FOR TEEN
VIZ media
viz.com
SHONEN JUMP
DRAGON BALL SUPER © 2015 by BIRD STUDIO, Toyotarou/SHUEISHA Inc.
DRAGON BALL SUPER
STORY BY Akira Toriyama
ART BY Toyotarou
1

STOP!

YOU'RE READING THE WRONG WAY!

★ ONE-PUNCH MAN READS FROM RIGHT TO LEFT, STARTING IN THE UPPER-RIGHT CORNER. JAPANESE IS READ FROM RIGHT TO LEFT, MEANING THAT ACTION, SOUND EFFECTS, AND WORD-BALLOON ORDER ARE COMPLETELY REVERSED FROM ENGLISH ORDER.